# Ten Poe
# about Love

Candlestick Press

Published by:
Candlestick Press,
Diversity House, 72 Nottingham Road, Arnold, Nottingham NG5 6LF
www.candlestickpress.co.uk

Design and typesetting by Craig Twigg

Printed by Ratcliff & Roper Print Group, Nottinghamshire, UK

Selection and Introduction © Lorraine Mariner, 2019

Cover illustration © Sara Boccaccini Meadows, 2019

Candlestick Press monogram © Barbara Shaw, 2008

© Candlestick Press, 2019

ISBN 978 1 907598 82 1

**Acknowledgements:**

The poems in this pamphlet are reprinted from the following books, all
by permission of the publishers listed unless stated otherwise. Every
effort has been made to trace the copyright holders of the poems
published in this book. The editor and publisher apologise if any material
has been included without permission or without the appropriate
acknowledgement, and would be glad to be told of anyone who has not
been consulted.

Thanks are due to all the copyright holders cited below for their kind
permission:

Fleur Adcock, *Collected Poems 1960-2000* (Bloodaxe Books, 2000)
www.bloodaxebooks.com. John Ashbery, *Collected Poems: 1956-1987*
ed. Mark Ford (Carcanet Press, 2003). ee cummings, *Complete Poems
1904-1962* edited by George J. Firmage (New York: Liveright, 1991),
copyright 1952, (c) 1980, 1991 by the Trustees for the E. E. Cummings
Trust, Used by permission of Liveright Publishing Corporation. Lorraine
Mariner, poem first published in this pamphlet. Tishani Doshi,
*Everything Begins Elsewhere* (Bloodaxe Books, 2016)
www.bloodaxebooks.com. Sinéad Morrissey, *The State of the Prisons*
(Carcanet Press, 2005). Peter Sansom, *Careful What You Wish For*
(Carcanet Press, 2015). RS Thomas, *Collected Later Poems: 1988-2000*
(Bloodaxe Books, 2004) www.bloodaxebooks.com.

All permissions cleared courtesy of Swift Permissions
(swiftpermissions@gmail.com).

Where poets are no longer living, their dates are given.

# Contents

,

# Introduction

Falling in love can be the thing which inspires someone to write
their first poem and set them off on the path to becoming a poet.
The National Poetry Library, where I work, has well over 200
anthologies on the theme of love, more than any other subject, so
I knew picking the poems for this selection was not going to be
easy. But I was up for the challenge as I'd get to share some of
my all-time favourite love poems.

I wanted to include some poems that could be read at a marriage
ceremony. Friends asked me to read 'i carry your heart with me'
by ee cummings at their wedding and I think what makes this
love poem so special is that there's something timeless about
it. At a wedding you want to express permanence and eternity
and Sinéad Morrissey's villanelle 'Genetics' manages to do this
whilst celebrating her own parents' failed marriage.

My own contribution is a poem written for my sister's wedding.
She described to me their first date walking along the Thames
and I decided to riff on Ewan MacColl's folk song 'Sweet
Thames, Flow Softly', though my sister was a bit concerned
about this because of that song's heartbroken ending! My choices
are not always entirely happy, but I think there is joy and honesty
in all of them.

Most of these poems are addressed to the object of the poet's
affection and that's the wonderful thing about love poems:
though they're the work of the poet they also belong to
somebody else, the person they were written for. And the best
love poems go on to become part of each reader's romantic life. I
hope some of these poems will become your poems.


*Lorraine Mariner*

## 92

i carry your heart with me(i carry it in
my heart)i am never without it(anywhere
i go you go,my dear;and whatever is done
by only me is your doing,my darling)
                                    i fear
no fate(for you are my fate,my sweet)i want
no world(for beautiful you are my world,my true)
and it's you are whatever a moon has always meant
and whatever a sun will always sing is you

here is the deepest secret nobody knows
(here is the root of the root and the bud of the bud
and the sky of the sky of a tree called life;which grows
higher than soul can hope or mind can hide)
and this is the wonder that's keeping the stars apart

i carry your heart(i carry it in my heart)


*ee cummings (1894 – 1962)*

## Marriage Morning

Light, so low upon earth,
  You send a flash to the sun.
Here is the golden close of love,
  All my wooing is done.
Oh, the woods and the meadows,
  Woods where we hid from the wet,
Stiles where we stay'd to be kind,
  Meadows in which we met!

Light, so low in the vale
  You flash and lighten afar,
For this is the golden morning of love,
  And you are his morning star.
Flash, I am coming, I come,
  By meadow and stile and wood,
Oh, lighten into my eyes and heart,
  Into my heart and my blood!

Heart, are you great enough
  For a love that never tires?
O heart, are you great enough for love?
  I have heard of thorns and briers.
Over the thorns and briers,
  Over the meadows and stiles,
Over the world to the end of it
  Flash for a million miles.


*Alfred, Lord Tennyson (1809 – 1892)*

## A Song of Love

Oh, drink thou deep of the purple wine,
   And it's hey for love, for I love you so!
Oh, clasp me close, with your lips on mine,
   And it's hey for love, for I love you so!
The sea lies violet, deep, and wide,
My heart beats high with the rushing tide;
Was it fancy, beloved, the seagulls cried:
   "Sing loud for love, for I love him so"?

Oh, little boat on the tossing wave,
   Sing loud for love, for I love him so!
Oh, tall pine tree in the shadows grave,
   Sing loud for love, for I love him so!
The little waves kiss the gleaming sand,
I laugh in the sun on the joyful land;
Beloved, one clasp of your strong young hand;
   The world is fair, for I love you so!

*Alice Moore Dunbar-Nelson (1875 – 1935)*

## A Straw Hat

On a hook by the window, with another
that the youngest grew out of. Here it is
knocked off by the wave I didn't see,
laughing, a mouth full of sea. But yours
where did it go, last-minute-anywhere-hot hat,
'hello' and 'thank you' all we could say
by the pool, or a dusty train into the mountains. Gone,
while this one persists, a real dad's hat,
under the tree he never had, the books
he never read, unravelling at the edge of shade, sweat
in the salt-stained band. I tip it back. Shoot me
if I wear it into town or a steady walk
to the pub. It bobs like a cork in the past
and present world, I take it off to you,
love of my life, light of my life, willing
to walk with me even in a hat like this.


*Peter Sansom*

## A Marriage

We met
    under a shower
of bird-notes.
    Fifty years passed,
love's moment
    in a world in
servitude to time.
    She was young:
I kissed with my eyes
    closed and opened
them on her wrinkles.
    'Come,' said death,
choosing her as his
    partner for
the last dance. And she,
    who in life
had done everything
    with a bird's grace,
opened her bill now
    for the shedding
of one sigh no
    heavier than a feather.


*RS Thomas (1913 – 2000)*

## Love Poem

Ultimately, we will lose each other
to something. I would hope for grand
circumstance – death or disaster.
But it might not be that way at all.
It might be that you walk out
one morning after making love
to buy cigarettes, and never return,
or I fall in love with another man.
It might be a slow drift into indifference.
Either way, we'll have to learn
to bear the weight of the eventuality
that we will lose each other to something.
So why not begin now, while your head
rests like a perfect moon in my lap,
and the dogs on the beach are howling?
Why not reach for the seam in this South Indian
night and tear it, just a little, so the falling
can begin? Because later, when we cross
each other on the streets, and are forced
to look away, when we've thrown
the disregarded pieces of our togetherness
into bedroom drawers and the smell
of our bodies is disappearing like the sweet
decay of lilies – what will we call it,
when it's no longer love?


*Tishani Doshi*

# Genetics

My father's in my fingers, but my mother's in my palms.
I lift them up and look at them with pleasure –
I know my parents made me by my hands.

They may have been repelled to separate lands,
to separate hemispheres, may sleep with other lovers,
but in me they touch where fingers link to palms.

With nothing left of their togetherness but friends
who quarry for their image by a river,
at least I know their marriage by my hands.

I shape a chapel where a steeple stands.
And when I turn it over,
my father's by my fingers, my mother's by my palms

demure before a priest reciting psalms.
My body is their marriage register.
I re-enact their wedding with my hands.

So take me with you, take up the skin's demands
for mirroring in bodies of the future.
I'll bequeath my fingers, if you bequeath your palms.
We know our parents make us by our hands.


*Sinéad Morrissey*

## Kissing

The young are walking on the riverbank,
arms around each other's waists and shoulders,
pretending to be looking at the waterlilies
and what might be a nest of some kind, over
there, which two who are clamped together
mouth to mouth have forgotten about.
The others, making courteous detours
around them, talk, stop talking, kiss.
They can see no one older than themselves.
It's their river. They've got all day.

Seeing's not everything. At this very
moment the middle-aged are kissing
in the backs of taxis, on the way
to airports and stations. Their mouths and tongues
are soft and powerful and as moist as ever.
Their hands are not inside each other's clothes
(because of the driver) but locked so tightly
together that it hurts: it may leave marks
on their not of course youthful skin, which they won't
notice. They too may have futures.


*Fleur Adcock*

## Some Trees

These are amazing: each
Joining a neighbor, as though speech
Were a still performance.
Arranging by chance

To meet as far this morning
From the world as agreeing
With it, you and I
Are suddenly what the trees try

To tell us we are:
That their merely being there
Means something; that soon
We may touch, love, explain.

And glad not to have invented
Such comeliness, we are surrounded:
A silence already filled with noises,
A canvas on which emerges

A chorus of smiles, a winter morning.
Placed in a puzzling light, and moving,
Our days put on such reticence
These accents seem their own defense.


*John Ashbery (1927 – 2017)*

## Meeting by the River

Let your hearts always
be meeting by the River
as they did on that first
wet February day

from hesitant "Hellos"
at Embankment Station
the Thames was urging
"This is the way".

The BT Tower whispered
"Keep on talking",
the NT concurred,
"There's so much to say!"

Waterloo Bridge insisted
"Keep on walking"
while the Festival Hall
had a Prelude to play.

The restaurant you ate in
raised its glasses,
the pub you got warm in
was murmuring "Stay",

Tate Modern's portraits
grinned on their canvases
and St. Paul's already knew
the promises you'd pray.

Let your hearts always
be meeting by the River
as they did on that first
wet February day.

*Lorraine Mariner*